PHYSICAL
SCIENCE
PROJECTS
★ for kids ★

A PROJECT GUIDE TO

MATTER

Claire O'Neal

Mitchell Lane

P.O. Box 196
Hockessin, Delaware 19707
Visit us on the web: www.mitchelllane.com
Comments? email us: mitchelllane@mitchelllane.com

Mitchell Lane

PHYSICAL SCIENCE PROJECTS
☆ for kids ☆

A Project Guide to:
Chemistry • Electricity and Magnetism
Forces and Motion • Light and Optics
Matter • Sound

Copyright © 2012 by Mitchell Lane Publishers

PUBLISHER'S NOTE: The facts on which this book
is based have been thoroughly researched.
Documentation of such research can be
found on page 44. While every possible effort
has been made to ensure accuracy, the
publisher will not assume liability for damages
caused by inaccuracies in the data, and
makes no warranty on the accuracy of the
information contained herein.

The Internet sites referenced herein were
active as of the publication date. Due to the
fleeting nature of some web sites, we cannot
guarantee they will all be active when you are
reading this book.

Library of Congress
Cataloging-in-Publication Data

O'Neal, Claire.
 A project guide to matter / Claire O'Neal.
     p. cm. — (Physical science projects for
kids)
 Includes bibliographical references and
index.
 ISBN 978-1-58415-967-4 (library bound)
 1. Matter—Properties—Juvenile literature.
 2. Chemistry—Experiments—Juvenile
literature. I. Title.
 QC173.16.O54 2011
 530—dc22

                                                         2011002758

eBook ISBN: 9781612281094

Printing   1   2   3   4   5   6   7   8   9

                                                                   PLB

CONTENTS

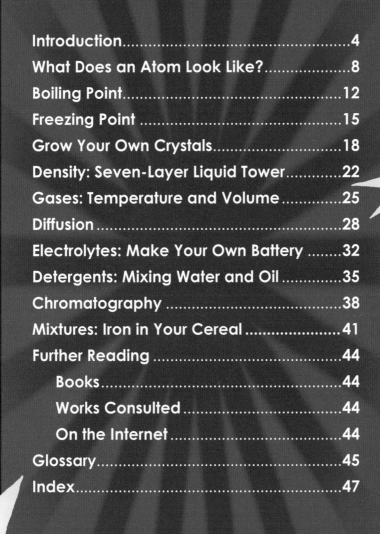

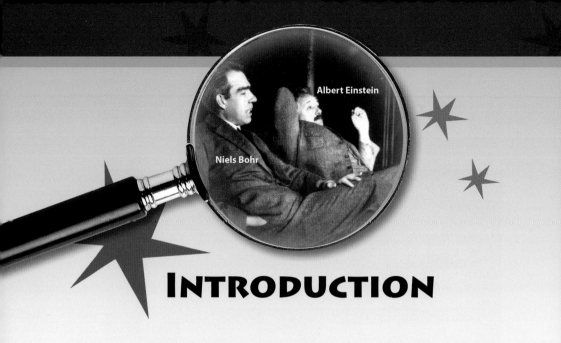

Albert Einstein

Niels Bohr

INTRODUCTION

Mysterious and invisible, atoms, the basic building blocks of the universe, have fascinated scientists for thousands of years. In the fourth century BCE, Greek philosopher Aristotle reasoned that every object had to be made out of something. He called this "something" matter. According to Aristotle, matter is anything that can be moved. Later, his definition was expanded: Matter is anything that takes up space and has mass.

In the nineteenth century, English physicist John Dalton showed that the smallest unbreakable unit of matter was the atom, far too small to see or feel. Since then, nuclear physicists have shown that one hydrogen atom is less than one billionth of a meter wide.

In the early twentieth century, scientists learned that even these building blocks have building blocks. Ernest Rutherford, Niels Bohr, and other physicists developed the theory of atomic structure. Their model showed a nucleus of protons and neutrons that was orbited by fast-moving electrons. Protons are positively charged, electrons are negatively charged, and neutrons are neutral. When an atom has the same number of protons and electrons, it is in a neutral state. An atom becomes charged when it gains or loses electrons. It can do this by interacting with other atoms or by entering a magnetic field.

Atoms can interact with one another to form larger groups called molecules. Sometimes all the atoms in a substance are the same. These pure substances, such as gold, silver, and oxygen, are called the elements. If different types of atoms interact, they form new substances. These compounds have entirely different properties from their components. Water, for example, is a compound made from molecules of two hydrogen atoms and one oxygen atom.

Also in the early 1900s, Albert Einstein showed that matter (or mass, m) was a trapped form of energy (E) in his famous equation $E = mc^2$. The letter c stands for the speed of light.) According to this equation, atoms hold enough stored energy to fuel a nuclear power plant or, in an atomic bomb, to level an entire city.

Scientists have discovered matter in five different forms.

In a **solid**, molecules are in a low-energy state—they are frozen, packed against each other. Solids have a regular, hard shape. When "freezing," the atoms in salt or diamonds pack in strict order close to each other to form crystals. Solids can be made of mixtures of pure substances. Many rocks, such as granite or limestone, are mixtures of more than one type of mineral.

In a **liquid**, molecules have more energy, slipping and sliding around and past one another. However, they do not escape the forces that hold them together. Gravity acts on liquids so that they fill containers, whether they are buckets or lakebeds. Liquids take up a definite volume that can be measured. Even though they move easily, they are difficult to compress, or squeeze into a smaller volume. Pistons in hydraulic systems use this property, applying pressure to liquids in order to do enormous amounts of work.

In **gases**, molecules are at a high state of energy. Gas molecules bump, whiz, and fly past one another. They seek to spread out from one another, occupying as much space as possible. Unlike solids or liquids, gases compress easily. Tanks of oxygen used for scuba diving and for hospital patients are filled with compressed air, as are air brakes that stop trains.

Fascinating discoveries have uncovered two more states of matter. The fourth state, **plasma**, was discovered in 1879. It is found in stars, where atoms have enough energy to turn their electrons into an electricity-conducting soup. Lightning is another example of plasma, and engineers have figured out how to use plasma in television sets

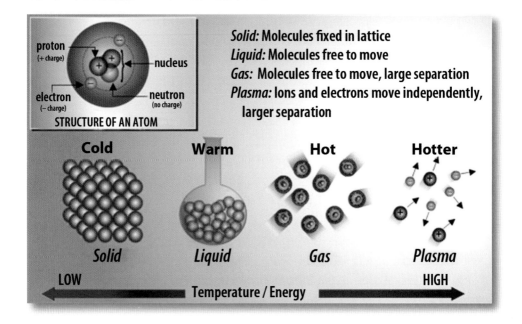

STRUCTURE OF AN ATOM

proton (+ charge)
nucleus
electron (– charge)
neutron (no charge)

Solid: Molecules fixed in lattice
Liquid: Molecules free to move
Gas: Molecules free to move, large separation
Plasma: Ions and electrons move independently, larger separation

Cold — Solid
Warm — Liquid
Hot — Gas
Hotter — Plasma

LOW ◄—— Temperature / Energy ——► HIGH

and other appliances. However, plasmas are hard to use in household experiments. Like gases, they do not have a definite shape. They are also unstable.

In 2001, scientists received the Nobel Prize for creating a sample of the fifth state of matter, called a **Bose-Einstein condensate**. In this state, gas molecules glob together to form a super-cold superatom. The state was named after Satyendra Nath Bose and Albert Einstein, who predicted the state after reading Bose's paper.

This book will look at the three states of matter commonly found on Earth: solids, liquids, and gases. Every element or compound has a special range of temperatures and pressures where it exists as one of these states of matter. Some types of matter, such as water, can be found in nature in all three states (as water ice, liquid water, and water vapor).

In this book, you'll find science project ideas to help you learn more about the structure and physical properties of matter, such as temperature, pressure, and density; how they are related; and how we can use these properties to do work. You'll find out about the electrical charges that are present in all types of matter, and how these help create or separate mixtures, solutions, and compounds. Whether for school or just for fun, you'll learn to think like a physicist while using

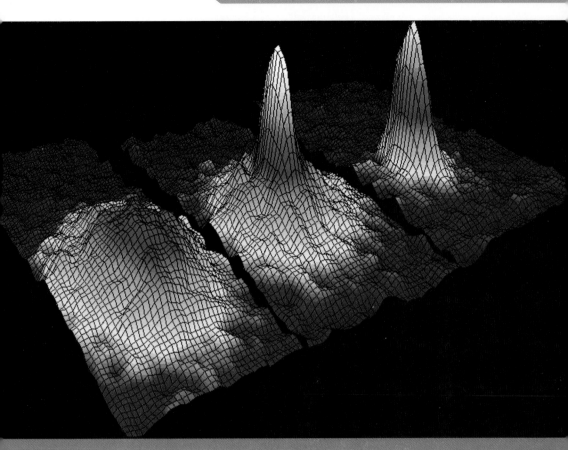

As a gas supercools under special conditions, it can form a Bose-Einstein condensate (seen in the right peak). Individual gas atoms clump together to become a dense blob (blue/white peaks), where the group of atoms behaves as one atom.

materials you probably already have at home. Follow these rules as you explore the structure and properties of matter:

1. Before starting any experiment, ask **an adult** for permission.
2. Read the instructions all the way through before you begin. Make sure you have all the materials you need, and that you understand the procedure.
3. Get a special notebook for keeping your notes and observations. Take careful notes when conducting your experiments.
4. Do not eat or drink anything from these experiments.

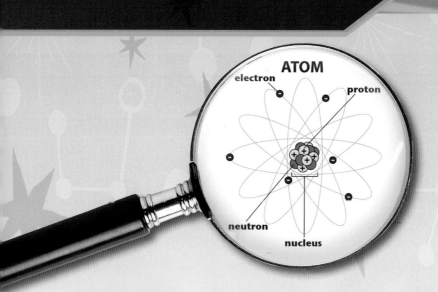

WHAT DOES AN ATOM LOOK LIKE?

Let's take a look inside the atom, the basic building block of matter. Every atom has a central core of positively charged protons and neutral neutrons. Tiny, negatively charged electrons orbit the core, like planets around a sun. This "solar system" model of the atom was used until the early 1900s. Then, Niels Bohr developed a more detailed model. He showed that electrons orbit at different levels or "shells," each with a different number of electrons. If the outer shell is full, the atom is fairly stable. If the outer shell is missing any electrons, it can easily combine with other atoms.

Scientists have improved upon the details of Bohr's model as well. However, the basic ideas behind the original solar system model remain useful for understanding atoms. Which element will you make in your solar system atom?

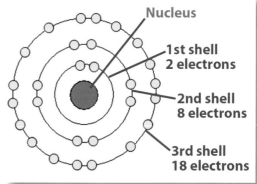

Periodic Table of the Elements

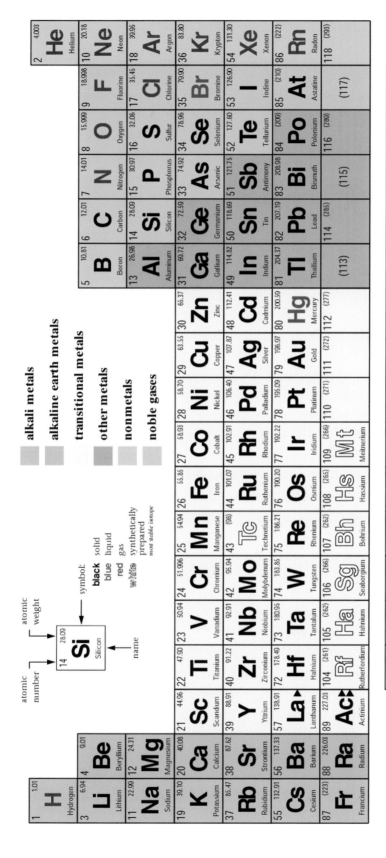

Materials
- Marbles in two different colors
- Plastic food wrap
- Yarn
- Wire coat hanger
- Pony beads
- Modeling clay

Instructions

1. Choose an atom from the periodic table of the elements (see page 9). Each element has an atomic number that determines its place in the table. An element's atomic number is equal to the number of protons in its nucleus. Every atom of hydrogen (H) has 1 proton; every atom of gold (AU) has 79.

2. Determine how many neutrons are in your atom by subtracting the number of protons from the element's mass number. You may not get a whole number because, unlike the number of protons, the number of neutrons in a nucleus can vary. The mass number on the periodic table represents an average weight of all of an element's isotopes—varieties with different numbers of neutrons. To find the number of neutrons to use for your model, round your result up or down.

3. Create your atom's nucleus. Count out marbles of one color to equal the number of protons from step 1, then count out marbles of the other color to equal the number of neutrons from step 2. Mix the marbles thoroughly and lay them in the center of two stacked sheets of plastic wrap. Bring the plastic wrap's edges up around the marbles to create a see-through sack. Securely tie the sack with yarn.

4. Use pony beads to represent the negatively charged electrons. Count out the same number of pony beads as the number of protons and set them aside.

5. Unwind the top of a wire hanger. Straighten the hanger so that it lies flat. Bend it into a smooth circle; this will be an orbit for your pony bead electrons. String the pony beads onto the circle, securing them at even intervals along the "orbit" using modeling clay. Twist the open ends of the wire tightly shut where they meet, entwining a piece of yarn into the joint.

6. Tie the nuclear sack to the other end of the yarn so that it is suspended in the center of the wire circle. Now your model shows

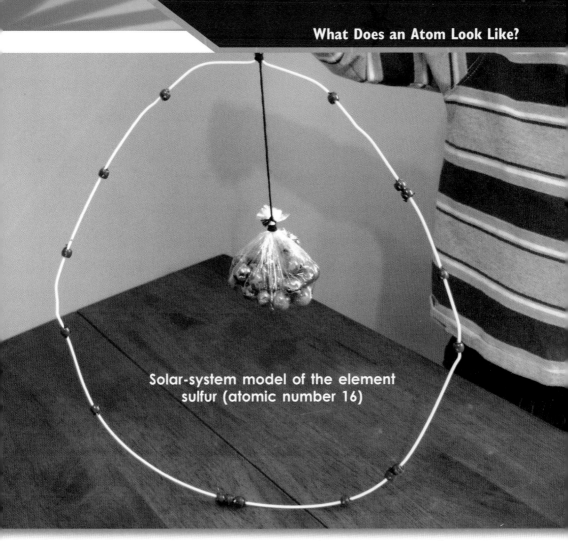

Solar-system model of the element
sulfur (atomic number 16)

the pony bead electrons orbiting around a nucleus of marble protons and neutrons. If you like, display your model from a plant hook, lamp, or nail for a picture frame, using another length of yarn if needed.

Take it further: Your model cannot possibly begin to describe the strangest property of an atom—its emptiness. Actual protons are 1,000 times larger than electrons, and the space between the nucleus and an electron's orbit is 50,000 times the size of a proton. For example, if your marble measures 15 millimeters across, then the pony-bead electron should only be 15 micrometers (15 millionths of a meter) across, or about 1/3 the width of a human hair. However, the electron would be orbiting 750 meters—almost half a mile—from the nucleus! Plot on a map of your neighborhood where your electrons should be.

BOILING POINT

Have you ever watched water boil in a pot? At first, tiny bubbles hover around the sides of the pot. The heat raises the energy of individual water molecules, making them move faster. As the temperature rises, the bonds that hold molecules of water together break. Some of the water turns to steam (a gas). Eventually, bubbles form faster and larger as the liquid water becomes high-energy gas. This point is called the boiling point.

Water is a good solvent, or dissolving agent, for certain compounds. When salts and sugar dissolve in water, they form solutions that strengthen the bonds between water molecules. Let's investigate the boiling point of water, and how different compounds affect it.

Materials
- 3 quarts (3 liters) of distilled water, divided
- 2-quart (2-liter) pot
- Candy or instant-read thermometer
- **An adult**
- Oven mitt
- Stove
- Timer
- Notebook and pencil
- ½ cup (125 milliliters) salt
- ½ cup (125 milliliters) white sugar
- Graph paper

Instructions

1. Pour 1 quart (1 liter) of distilled water into a pot. Clip the thermometer to the inside of the pot so that the tip is immersed in the water and not touching the pot wall.
2. With **an adult's** help, place the pot on the stove and turn the burner to medium. Start the timer.

Candy thermometers record very high temperatures—up to 400°F (200°C).

Sugar water gets very hot.
Be sure to work with an adult.

3. Read and record the temperature every 15 seconds until three readings of the same temperature are recorded. Take notes about your observations of the water.
4. **Ask the adult** to empty the pot (using an oven mitt), then add a fresh quart of distilled water. This time, stir in ½ cup salt before clipping the thermometer in place.
5. Repeat steps 2 and 3.
6. Repeat step 4, but this time use ½ cup white sugar instead of the salt.
7. Graph your results for all three boiling experiments, placing time on the x-axis and temperature on the y-axis. How do they compare? Why do you think the dissolved salt and sugar affect the boiling point?

Take it further: Find the boiling points of different solutions. You can use different amounts of solute, or make entirely different solutions from other common kitchen substances, such as baking soda, Epsom salts, cream of tartar, juices, vinegar, or food dye.

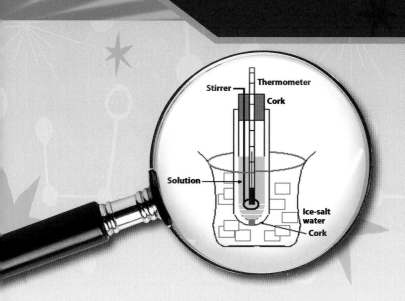

FREEZING POINT

While freezing is certainly less dramatic than boiling, the same forces control both types of change. Adding heat to water increases the energy in water molecules, making them move faster and spread apart. Removing heat from water removes energy from the molecules in the liquid, causing them to move less and to pack together, forming a solid. Let's look closely at how water and water solutions freeze.

Materials
- Distilled water
- Ice cube tray
- Freezer
- Quart-sized glass jar
- Thermometer
- Bowl, big enough to hold the jar
- Tap-water ice
- Rock salt
- Spoon
- Table salt
- Sugar

1. Fill an ice cube tray with distilled water and leave it in the freezer overnight.
2. Empty enough distilled-water ice cubes into the jar to fill it halfway. Add distilled water to the jar to make the ice just start to float. Place the thermometer in the jar and record the temperature.
3. Place the experiment jar in the bowl. Surround the bowl with regular-water ice and rock salt.
4. Stir the ice water in the jar with a spoon, then read and record the temperature every 30 seconds until three readings of the same temperature are recorded. Take notes about your observations of the water. Keep an eye on the outer bowl and add more rock salt and ice as it melts.

Water usually freezes at 32°F (0°C). Will adding rock salt or sugar change this freezing point?

5. Empty the jar and repeat step 2. Dissolve as much table salt as possible in the jar of water, noting the amount of salt you used. Repeat steps 3 and 4.
6. Repeat step 5, but use sugar instead of table salt.
7. Graph your results for all three freezing experiments, placing time on the *x*-axis and temperature on the y-axis. How do they compare? Why do you think the dissolved salt and sugar affect the freezing point?

Take it further: An old wives' tale says that hot water freezes faster than cold water. Design an experiment to test this claim.

GROW YOUR OWN CRYSTALS

In nature, many solids form not from freezing, but from being left behind during evaporation. Dissolved minerals and compounds change into beautiful crystals when their solute, or the liquid surrounding them, slowly evaporates. Molecules pack together to create a growing crystal. Each molecule orients itself so that its shape lines up tightly with its neighbor. Like little magnets, positively charged sites match up with negatively charged sites. This arrangement determines what shape the final crystal will be. From proud sprays of quartz columns to small, brilliant diamonds, the results can be stunning.

Growing your own crystals is fun and easy. The following recipe produces a lot of thin crystals almost immediately.

Materials
- Epsom salts (magnesium sulfate)
- Warm water
- Measuring cup
- Spoon
- Dark construction paper
- Baking pan, 9 inches by 13 inches, or broiler pan
- Table salt (sodium chloride)
- White sugar (sucrose)
- Clock

Growing Thin Crystals
Instructions
1. Add 1 tablespoon Epsom salts to ¼ cup warm water and stir until completely dissolved.
2. Lay the construction paper flat in the bottom of the pan.
3. Gently pour the salt solution onto the construction paper. Set the pan somewhere flat, still, and quiet, such as an empty countertop or a sunny porch step.
4. Check the pan once every hour and record your observations. What is happening to the solution? What is forming on the paper?
5. Repeat the experiment using different concentrations of Epsom salts, such as 1 teaspoon or 2 teaspoons to each ¼ cup water. How do the results differ? Vary the compound you want to crystallize, using table salt or white sugar. What do their crystals look like? How long do they take to form?

Epsom salts will form thin crystals in warm water.

Growing Large Crystals

With a little more patience and time, you can grow crystals that are large in all three dimensions. Just choose one of many pure household substances.

Materials
- Pure compound—Examples: table salt (sodium chloride), white sugar (sucrose), Epsom salts (magnesium sulfate), alum (potassium aluminum sulfate), copper sulfate (algaecide, available in aquarium stores)
- Measuring spoons
- Hot water
- Glass jar with screw-top lid
- Tweezers
- Plate
- Fishing line
- Pencil
- Hammer
- Nail

Instructions
1. With **an adult's** help, add ¼ teaspoon of your desired compound to 1 cup of hot water and stir until completely dissolved. Add more compound, ¼ teaspoon at a time, stirring after each addition, until no more dissolves. At this point, you have created a supersaturated solution. So many molecules of your compound (the solute) are dissolved in the water (the solvent) that there is literally no room for any more.
2. Carefully pour the hot solution into a very clean glass jar, leaving any undissolved particles behind. Screw a clean lid onto the jar and allow it to cool.
3. When the outside of the jar feels cool, unscrew the cap. Use a clean spoon to sprinkle a few more crystals of your compound into the jar. Do not stir. These seed crystals encourage dissolved molecules of the compound to build the crystal lattice—the pattern the crystal

will follow. Repeat this step twice a day until you see crystals bigger than the grains you introduce.

4. Use very clean tweezers to remove one or two small crystals from the jar to a clean plate. Tie a crystal securely with fishing line. Meanwhile, have **an adult** help you poke a hole through the top of the lid using a hammer and nail. Thread the free end of the fishing line through the hole, tying it to a pencil to keep it from

A supersaturated solution

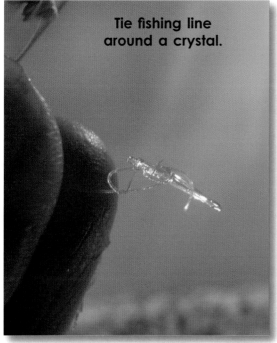

Tie fishing line around a crystal.

slipping back through. Lower the tied crystal back into the super-saturated solution and screw on the top. Adjust the length of the fishing line, if necessary, so that the crystal hangs sus-pended in the liquid.

5. Place the jar in a quiet place where it can sit undisturbed. Wait and watch, taking pictures if you like to monitor the crystal's growth.

DENSITY: SEVEN-LAYER LIQUID TOWER

Hold a Styrofoam packing peanut in one hand and a peanut-sized rock in the other. Why is the rock heavier, even though both objects are the same size? The answer lies in their density. Over the same volume, rocks pack in a lot more mass than Styrofoam, which is mostly air. The rock is denser. Not all rocks and minerals are built the same, however. Lead is four times heavier than aluminum, for example. The atomic structure of lead allows it to pack more atoms in a given volume than aluminum.

You've seen density at work in liquids, too. In salad dressing, oil floats on top of vinegar. Thick honey sinks to the bottom of a glass of watery tea. Using liquids you probably already have in your kitchen, you can compare density in liquids and create a spectacular seven-layer tower.

Instructions
1. Pour a little corn syrup, water, and rubbing alcohol into separate cups. Add a few drops of food coloring to each, coloring them differently.

Materials

- 3 colors of food coloring
- Cups or glasses
- Light corn syrup
- Water
- Rubbing alcohol
- Honey
- Colored dish soap
- Vegetable oil
- Baby oil
- Measuring cups and spoons
- Graduated cylinder or a straight-sided drinking glass or container

2. Test the seven liquids to see which is denser. Testing two at a time, add 1 tablespoon of each liquid to a glass, noting which liquid forms the top layer and which layer sinks to the bottom. For example, pour the rubbing alcohol in the glass, and then drizzle honey on top of it. Which sinks, and which floats? Comparing the liquids two at a time, can you figure out how they should stack up from most to least dense?

3. Make the seven-layer liquid tower, measuring ¼ cup of each substance and pouring it into the graduated cylinder from most dense to least dense. Pour each layer against the inside of the glass to let the liquid settle slowly.

    Add layers in the following order:

       Layer 1: honey
       Layer 2: corn syrup
       Layer 3: dish soap
       Layer 4: water
       Layer 5: vegetable oil
       Layer 6: rubbing alcohol
       Layer 7: lamp oil

4. Density is expressed as mass divided by volume. For comparison, water has a density of 1. Compare these numbers with your findings from step 2.

Using food coloring in the different liquids will make your column more dramatic.

Why do these liquids stack on top of each other? What would happen if you poured them into the column in a different order?

Take it further: You can also make a density column using sugar and water. Add increasing amounts of sugar to small glasses of water. Color each solution differently with food coloring. Layer the solutions carefully on top of each other as you did above, with the highest sugar content solution on the bottom and the lowest at the top. Over time, these solutions will mix. How long does it take for the layers to break up?

GASES: TEMPERATURE AND VOLUME

You may not think much about the structure of air. After all, it's invisible! But capture air in a balloon and you can see that air is matter just like any other substance—it has weight, and it takes up space. Gas molecules spread out to fill the balloon by bumping into and bouncing off one another. How fast they go is governed by kinetic energy, the energy of motion.

Did you know that temperature is actually a measure of kinetic energy? At high temperatures, gases have more energy, and their molecules move around faster. Hot-air balloons float through the sky by heating regular air with fire to make it expand. When it expands enough, it becomes less dense than the air outside the balloon and will rise. In contrast, at lower temperatures, gases have less energy. Gas molecules move around and collide less, taking up less space. On a cold day, car tires become underinflated because the gas inside them has less energy to push against the tire walls. More air has to be added to the tires to bring them back to their proper pressure.

Materials
- 3 similar balloons
- Handheld bicycle pump (optional)
- Fabric tape measure
- permanent marker
- Refrigerator or freezer
- Laundry basket or box
- Source of heat (a lamp, a heater, a car)
- Thermometer with Celsius scale

WARNING: Stay out of hot cars. Your balloon will be fine in there by itself.

Instructions

1. Blow up three balloons to roughly equal size. To be really precise, use a bicycle pump and inflate the balloons using the same number of pumps. Measure the distance around each balloon in millimeters at its widest point. Write that number on the balloon. This measurement is the balloon's starting circumference.
2. Label one balloon COLD. Place it in the refrigerator or freezer.
3. Label a second balloon ROOM TEMPERATURE. Place it under a laundry basket (so that it can't escape) on a table or on a bed—somewhere away from direct contact with heaters or air conditioners.

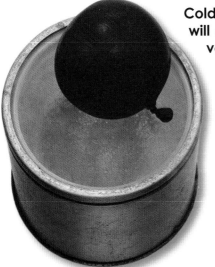

Cold temperatures will decrease the volume of a balloon.

Start with balloons that are all
the same size and shape.

4. Label the third balloon HOT. Place it inside a hot car or near (not touching) a heat source such as a lamp or a heater. Record the air temperature (in degrees Celsius) at each balloon's location.
5. Wait one hour to allow energy (heat) exchange between the gas inside the balloon and its new surroundings.
6. Working quickly, remove the balloon from the freezer and measure its circumference now. Write the new circumference on the balloon under the first measurement.
7. Repeat step 4 for the other two balloons.
8. Find the change in circumference for each balloon by subtracting the starting measurement from the ending one. (NOTE: For the old balloon, you should get a negative number.) How did the temperature affect the volume of the gas inside the balloons?

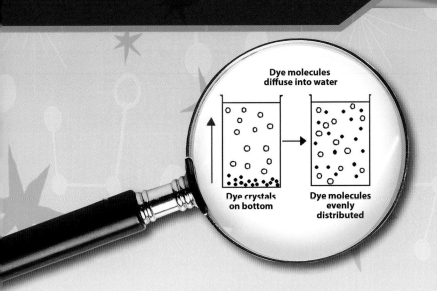

Dye molecules
diffuse into water

Dye crystals
on bottom

Dye molecules
evenly
distributed

DIFFUSION

Unlike molecules in the solid state, molecules in the gas or liquid state can move randomly in all directions, bouncing around and into one another. They must spread out to occupy all possible space evenly within a system. This process is called diffusion.

Our sense of smell relies on the property of diffusion. Many types of matter, such as fresh-baked cookies and rotting garbage, give off gas molecules, called volatiles, that diffuse through the air. When they reach our nose, we detect an odor. Like all gas molecules, volatiles obey diffusion by moving from an area with many volatile molecules—the source of the smell—to an area with few volatile molecules, such as the outside air. How fast do they move? Let's find out!

Materials
- A friend
- Strong-smelling object in a container with a lid, such as a jar filled with ground coffee or a scented candle
- Timer
- Metric tape measure
- Calculator
- Graph paper

In Air

Instructions

1. Place a smelly object in the middle of a room. Have your friend stand in a room nearby.
2. Open the lid and start the timer. When your friend says he or she can smell the object, stop the timer and record its reading in seconds.
3. Measure how far the scent had to travel in meters.

How long will it take for the boy in red to smell the coffee?

4. To determine the speed of this scent's diffusion, divide the distance by the time.

How fast did the scent travel?

5. Repeat the experiment several times, each time with your friend standing slightly farther away. Make a graph, plotting the distance the scent had to travel on the x-axis against time on the y-axis. If the graph makes a straight line, the scent travels at a constant speed as it diffuses. However, you are more likely to see a curve, showing that the scent slows down as it spreads out.

6. Repeat the experiment with different smelly objects. Be creative! Given the same temperature and pressure, the diffusion speeds of different objects should be the same. Is this true?

In Liquid

What does diffusion look like in a liquid? It's easy to see with water and food coloring. Check it out!

Materials	
♦ Quart- or liter-sized glass or jar	♦ Timer
	♦ Ice
♦ Water	♦ **An adult**
♦ Food coloring	♦ Microwave
	♦ Oven mitts

1. Fill the glass jar with water. Add a single drop of food coloring and start the timer. Watch the color as it spreads out through the water. Stop the timer when the color is evenly spread out.

2. Repeat the experiment with food coloring in ice water. Is diffusion in cold water faster or slower than in warm water?

Keep the temperature of the food coloring the same. Try to add just one drop in each jar of water.

3. With **an adult's** help, repeat the experiment with a jar of water that has been heated to boiling in the microwave. (Be sure to wear oven mitts.) How does the rate of diffusion in hot water compare to the rate in warm water and in ice water?

ELECTROLYTES: MAKE YOUR OWN BATTERY

Because of the charges held by protons and electrons, all matter holds potential electricity. When salts dissolve in water, their molecules split apart into smaller particles called ions that carry positive and negative charges. Salts are called electrolytes because a salt solution can conduct electricity. Salt water may look like ordinary water from the outside, but inside, salt ions form a web of electricity with water molecules. Household batteries actually use electrolytes to create electricity.

Like most vegetables, the potato is mostly water. When growing, potatoes take up phosphate ions from the soil. Those ions dissolve in water inside the potato to become phosphoric acid, an excellent electrolyte. Lemons contain citric acid, another good electrolyte. Just think—sitting on your pantry shelf, you have two batteries waiting to happen!

The power in a "lemon battery" can be measured by a voltmeter.

Materials
- Potato
- **An adult**
- Knife
- 2 plates
- 4 pennies
- Steel wool
- 4 galvanized steel nails
- 6 wires with alligator clips
- 2 small flashlight bulbs or small LED bulbs
- Lemon

Instructions
1. With **an adult's** help, cut a potato in half. Place the halves flat-side down on a plate.
2. Polish two pennies with a piece of steel wool until they are very clean and shiny. Cut a small slit on the side of each potato half and push a polished penny about two-thirds of the way into each slit.

If you use two whole potatoes instead of halves, use a tray to keep the potatoes from rolling away.

The copper in the pennies will react with the phosphoric acid in the potatoes to make electrons available, creating the anode (negative end) of the battery.

3. Push one nail into each potato half so that the top of the nail sticks out at least ½ inch. The nails serve as the cathode (positive end) of the battery. Be sure that the nails and pennies do not touch.

4. Connect your battery using three alligator clips. Wire 1: Attach one clip to the nail on potato half A, the other to the penny on potato half B. Wire 2: Attach one clip to the nail on potato half B. Wire 3: Attach one end to the penny on potato half A.

5. Touch or clip the two free ends against the metal bottom of a flashlight bulb or LED bulb. What happens?

6. Repeat steps 1–5 with the lemon. Compare how bright the bulb gets between the two batteries. Which conducts electricity better, a potato-powered battery or a lemon-powered battery? Why?

Acid (such as vinegar) is an electrolyte and will also light the bulb.

Take it further: You can make a stronger battery by connecting several potato or lemon halves in series. Use a voltmeter, available at hardware stores, to measure your battery's power. Can you make a battery out of a glass of salt water? A glass of cola?

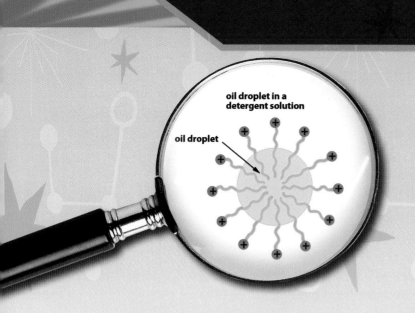

oil droplet in a
detergent solution

oil droplet

DETERGENTS: MIXING WATER AND OIL

While water readily dissolves many compounds, it can't dissolve everything. Take salad dressing, for example. Vinegar, a water solution, will not permanently mix with oil. At the atomic level, it makes perfect sense. Oil molecules—made of hydrogen and carbon atoms—are nonpolar. The hydrogen and carbon atoms bond together so that they share electrons evenly. Water molecules, on the other hand, are polar. Water's oxygen atom pulls electrons away from its partner hydrogen atoms. This unequal sharing turns the water molecule into a mini-magnet, with oxygen at the negative end and hydrogen at the positive end.

Oil and water will never mix on their own, but they can form an emulsion—a smooth mixture of liquids that do not normally stay mixed —with help from detergents. Ever wonder how detergents help clean your pots and pans? Detergents have nonpolar tails that attract nonpolar oils, like grease. Meanwhile, their small, polar heads interact with polar water. When the water flows off the pan, it pulls the detergent with it. The detergent pulls the oil, and all three go down the drain.

Explore the properties of different detergents with the following experiment. Test household soaps to see which ones work best.

Materials
- 6 quart-sized glass jars with screw-top lids
- Masking tape
- Marker
- Glass measuring cup
- Water
- Food coloring
- Cooking oil
- Liquid dishwashing detergent
- Liquid hand soap
- Liquid laundry detergent
- 1 raw egg yolk, stirred with a fork

Instructions
1. Using masking tape and a marker, label six jars as follows: 1: control; 2: dish soap; 3. liquid hand soap; 4. laundry detergent; 5. raw egg yolk.
2. Fill each jar with 1 cup of water. Add a few drops of food coloring, shaking gently until mixed thoroughly.
3. Tilt each jar slightly. Slowly pour ½ cup oil down the inside of the jar so that you are not pouring the oil directly onto the surface of the water. Set the jars down. What are the liquids doing?

The jars should look the same before you add the detergents.

When you add the detergents, watch how they break up the oil.

Control — Softsoap-hand soap — Joy - dish soap — Tide - laundry soap

4. To jars 2 through 5, add a teaspoon of dish soap, hand soap, laundry soap, or raw egg yolk in the corresponding jar.
5. Cap all five jars and shake them thoroughly.

What happened to the oil and water layers? What mixture made the best emulsion, where the water and oil look to be the most evenly mixed? Take notes, and take or draw pictures of your experiment.

Take it further: Test "ultra" dish soap or laundry detergents, which manufacturers claim are more concentrated than regular brands. Can you use less detergent to get the same results? How well did the egg yolk work as a detergent? If you've ever had mayonnaise, you've tasted an emulsion of oil and water using egg yolk!

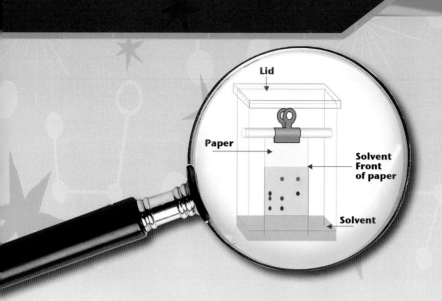

Lid

Paper

Solvent Front of paper

Solvent

CHROMATOGRAPHY

Chromatography is a process for separating mixtures. Crime scene investigators use chromatography every day to perform drug testing or to analyze evidence samples. Blood and urine, for example, are complex solutions of many dissolved compounds. Chromatography can separate each component from its compound based on how well it dissolves in a liquid. The components can then be identified.

This important technique was invented in the 1900s. Russian scientist Mikhail S. Tswett found that, when he dabbed ground-up leaves on filter paper and dipped the paper in a solvent, hidden pigments (colors) spread out along the filter paper as the solvent traveled. Tswett reasoned that the pigments moved because they could dissolve, at least partway, in the solvent. The easier a compound dissolves, the farther it will travel up the filter paper. With the experiment below, you can perform your own kitchen investigation on red pigments to uncover what really makes red, well, red.

Instructions

1. Set out one filter strip per sample, plus one extra. Make a line across each strip with the pencil, approximately one inch from the bottom. Label the strip at the bottom with the sample name (such as FOOD COLORING). Label the extra CONTROL.

38

Materials
- White coffee filters, cut into 1-inch strips
- Pencil
- Red fruit, such as cranberries, cherries, or strawberries
- Red cabbage
- Red candy, such as Twizzlers or Red Hots
- Red marker
- Red food coloring
- Bowls
- Spoon
- Baking sheet
- Toothpicks
- Drinking glasses
- Rubbing alcohol
- Clock
- Tape measure or ruler
- Nail polish remover
- Water

2. Apply each sample of red pigment to its strip by dipping a clean toothpick in the sample and rubbing the toothpick neatly along the pencil line. Grind up solid samples in separate bowls using a spoon, and use a clean toothpick to rub some of the ground-up solid along the pencil line. Lay all the strips flat on a baking sheet until completely dry.

3. Set out as many glasses as you have strips. Add ½ inch of rubbing alcohol to each glass. Rubbing alcohol is a mixture of alcohols. Alcohols are polar solvents, but they are not as strongly polar as water.

4. Set each filter strip in a glass, with the red pigment near the alcohol but not touching it. As the alcohol travels up the strips, watch its progress and note what you see.

Watch as the colors start to change.

How far does each pigment travel?

5. After 30 minutes, remove the strips from the glasses and lay them out to dry on a baking sheet. Measure how far each band has traveled from the starting line, noting the number of bands and their relative thickness. Are the red pigments the same?
6. Repeat the experiment using nail polish remover instead of rubbing alcohol. Nail polish remover is made of acetone, a common solvent used in chemistry. Acetone is also a polar solvent, but with different properties than water or alcohol.
7. Repeat the experiment using water.
8. Compare the chromatography strips of the same samples in different solvents. Which bands travel farther in which solvents? Compare strips using only one solvent and see if you can find pigments that match—bands that look the same and traveled about the same distance from the starting line.

Take it further: Use different food colorings instead of red, or highly colored fruits and vegetables, like blueberries, spinach, and carrots.

MIXTURES: IRON IN YOUR CEREAL

Mixtures aren't just found in liquids. Many rocks, such as granite, are mixtures of minerals. In some mixtures, each compound is clearly visible, and sometimes they can be separated. Many people enjoy eating a mixture every morning—cereal. On their own, breakfast cereals usually have some fiber, B vitamins, and lots of sugar. To help children and adults get the nutrition they need, many cereal manufacturers add vitamins and minerals to the cereal batter before baking. You can look for these compounds on the nutrition facts panel on the side of the box, and also in the ingredients list.

One mineral that is popularly added to cereal is iron. People need iron to help red blood cells carry oxygen throughout the body. People with low levels of iron in their blood suffer from anemia, causing them to feel weak, dizzy, and sleepy because their cells are starved of oxygen. While other vitamins and minerals dissolve in the cereal batter, iron is added as visible shavings, large enough to be seen with a magnifying glass. Acids in your stomach dissolve these shavings into a form your body can use.

How much iron is in your cereal? Let's find out!

Materials

- 3 types of breakfast cereal
- Paper towels
- Magnifying glass
- 1-cup measure
- Blender
- Water
- Magnet strong enough to pick up 10 or more paper clips
- Butter knife
- Glass jar
- Vinegar

Instructions

1. Choose three breakfast cereals that have significant, but different, amounts of iron, according to the nutrition facts panel on the side. For example, Total whole-wheat cereal has 100 percent of the recommended daily intake (RDI) for iron; Cheerios oat cereal has 49 percent. Pick a third cereal that has less than 10 percent RDI for iron, such as old-fashioned oats.

2. For cereal #1: Measure 1 cup of cereal and dump it onto a paper towel. Examine the cereal pieces with a magnifying glass. Do you see any dark flecks or spots? Hold the magnet up to the cereal. What happens? When you remove the magnet, can you see small iron pieces on it?

3. For cereal #1: Add the measured cereal and 5 cups of water to a blender. Blend on high for several minutes, or until the cereal is completely pulverized.

4. Remove the blender from its stand, gently shaking the blender to suspend the cereal particles. Dunk the

Cereal, magnified

magnet to the bottom of the liquid and bring it back up. Repeat the dunking four more times.

Roll up your sleeves before dunking the magnet in the cereal slurry.

5. Examine the magnet with the magnifying glass. Use the back of a butter knife to scrape the iron shavings you collect onto a paper towel. Label the paper towel with the cereal's name.
6. Thoroughly clean the measuring cup, magnet, and blender. Repeat the experiment for the other two cereals, using clean paper towels for each.
7. How does the iron content of the cereals compare? Did you get the results you would expect, given what you read on the nutrition labels?
8. To see how your stomach treats this iron, transfer all the shavings you collected to a clean glass jar. Fill the jar with vinegar and leave it overnight, or even for a few days. Watch how the shavings change. The acid in the vinegar (pH 4–5) is much weaker than your stomach acid (pH 1–2), but it does the same job. It strips electrons from the iron to make ions your body can use.

Books

Dingle, Adrian. *The Periodic Table: Elements With Style!* New York: Kingfisher, 2007.

Gardner, Robert. *Chemistry Science Fair Projects.* Berkeley Heights, NJ: Enslow Publishers, Inc., 2004.

Newmark, Ann. *Chemistry.* New York: DK Publishing, 2005.

Vecchione, Glen. *100 Amazing Award-Winning Science Fair Projects.* New York: Sterling Publishing Co, Inc., 2005.

———. *100 Amazing Make-It-Yourself Science Fair Projects.* New York: Sterling Publishing Co, Inc., 2005.

Winston, Robert. *It's Elementary!* New York: DK Publishing, 2007.

Works Consulted

"The Bohr Model." http://csep10.phys.utk.edu/astr162/lect/light/bohr.html

Brock, William H. *The Norton History of Chemistry.* New York: W.W. Norton & Company, Inc., 1993.

Chang, Raymond. *Chemistry.* New York: McGraw-Hill, Inc., 1994.

Cobb, Cathy, and Harold Goldwhite. *Creations of Fire: Chemistry's Lively History from Alchemy to the Atomic Age.* New York: Plenum Press, 1995.

Kiernan, Denise, and Joseph D'Agnese. *Science 101: Chemistry.* Irving, NY: Hydra Publishing, 2007.

Moore, John T. *Chemistry for Dummies.* Hoboken, NJ: Wiley Publishing, Inc., 2003.

Voet, Donald, and Judith G. Voet. *Biochemistry.* Somerset, NJ: John Wiley & Sons, 1995.

On the Internet

American Chemical Society—Science for Kids http://portal.acs.org/portal/acs/corg/content?_nfpb=true&_pageLabel=PP_TRANSITIONMAIN&node_id=878&use_sec=false&sec_url_var=region1&__uuid=5b0318f0-cbb7-44eb-ae96-406ffa11e766

Chemistry—An Introduction
    http://www.mcwdn.org/chemist/chemist.html
Gagnon, Steve. "All About Atoms." Jefferson Lab—Science Education.
    http://education.jlab.org/atomtour/listofparticles.html
    ———. "How Do I Make a Model of an Atom?" Jefferson Lab—Science
    Education. http://education.jlab.org/qa/atom_model.html
PBS: A Science Odyssey—Atom Builder
    http://www.pbs.org/wgbh/aso/tryit/atom/
PBS Kids Zoom! How to Make a Potato Battery
    http://pbskids.org/zoom/activities/phenom/potatobattery.html
Rader's Chem 4 Kids
    http://www.chem4kids.com/
University of Nottingham—The Periodic Table of Videos
    http://www.periodicvideos.com/

GLOSSARY

atom (AT-um)—The smallest unit of an element.

atomic number (uh-TAH-mik NUM-bur)—The number of protons found in the nucleus of an atom. All atoms of the same element share an atomic number.

boiling point (BOY-ling POYNT)—The temperature at which an element changes state, from a liquid to a gas.

bond (BOND)—A chemical attraction between atoms.

Bose-Einstein condensate (BOWS-EYN-steyn kon-DEN-sayt)—A solid-like state of matter where a gas has been cooled rapidly to temperatures near absolute zero.

chromatography (kroh-muh-TAH-gruh-fee)—A technique that separates compounds based on their chemical properties, such as their ability to dissolve in a solute.

compound (KOM-pownd)—A chemical made from one or more elements.

density (DEN-sih-tee)—The amount of mass in a given volume.

electrolyte (ee-LEK-troh-lyt)—A compound that separates into its component ions in solution.

element (EL-uh-munt)—A chemical substance that cannot be separated into simpler substances by ordinary chemical means.

emulsion (ee-MUL-shun)—A mixture of unmixable liquids.

evaporation (ee-vah-puh-RAY-shun)—Changing state from a liquid to a gas at temperatures below the boiling point.

freezing point (FREE-zing POYNT)—The temperature at which an element changes state, from a liquid to a solid.

gas—A high-energy state of matter where atoms can move freely.

ion (I-on)—A particle with an electric charge.

kinetic energy (kih-NEH-tik EH-nur-jee)—Energy of motion.

lattice (LAA-tis)—A regular arrangement of atoms that, on a large scale, makes an ordered crystal.

liquid (LIH-kwid)—A medium-energy state of matter where molecules can move more freely than in a solid, but less freely than in a gas.

mass number (MASS NUM-ber)—The average mass of an atom of a given element, reported on the periodic table.

molecule (MAH-leh-kyool)—The smallest unit of a compound. Molecules can be further divided into atoms.

nonpolar (non-POH-lur)—Lacking overall electric charge.

plasma (PLAZ-muh)—A state of matter where electrons move freely among atoms. Rare on earth, but the most common state of matter in space.

polar (POH-lur)—Carrying an overall electric charge.

seed crystal (SEED KRIH-stul)—A microscopic crystal that attracts ordered molecules to build a larger crystal.

solid (SAH-lid)—A low-energy state of matter that does not change size or shape.

solute (SAHL-yute)—A solid substance that can dissolve in a solvent.

solution (suh-LOO-shun)—An even mixture of a solvent and a dissolved solute.

solvent (SOL-vunt)— A liquid that can dissolve solid compounds.

supersaturated (soo-per-SAT-chur-ay-ted)—A solution containing the maximum possible amount of dissolved material.

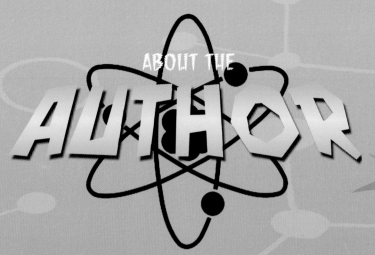

ABOUT THE
AUTHOR

Former biochemist Claire O'Neal has published over a dozen books with Mitchell Lane, including *A Project Guide to Rocks and Minerals, A Project Guide to Earthquakes, A Project Guide to Volcanoes, Exploring Earth's Biomes,* and *Projects in Genetics.* She holds degrees in English and Biology from Indiana University, and a Ph.D. in Chemistry from the University of Washington. She lives in Delaware with her husband, two young sons, and a fat black cat.